EXPLORING CIVIL RIGHTS

THE RISE

1967

JAY LESLIE

Franklin Watts®

An imprint of Scholastic Inc.

Content Consultant

A special thank you to Ryan M. Jones at the
National Civil Rights Museum for his expert consultation.

Library of Congress Cataloging-in-Publication Data
Names: Leslie, Jay, author.
Title: The rise: 1967 / by Jay Leslie.
Other titles: Exploring civil rights.
Description: First edition. | New York : Franklin Watts, an imprint of
   Scholastic Inc., 2023. | Series: Exploring civil rights | Includes
   bibliographical references and index. | Audience: Ages 10–14 | Audience:
   Grades 7–9 | Summary: "Series continuation. Narrative nonfiction, key
   events of the Civil Rights Movement in the years after 1965. Photographs
   throughout"—Provided by publisher.
Identifiers: LCCN 2022039916 (print) | LCCN 2022039917 (ebook) |
   ISBN 9781338837520 (library binding) | ISBN 9781338837537 (paperback) |
   ISBN 9781338837544 (ebk)
Subjects: LCSH: African Americans—Civil rights—History—20th
   century—Juvenile literature. | Civil rights movements—United
   States—History—20th century—Juvenile literature. | Civil rights
   workers—United States—Juvenile literature. | BISAC: JUVENILE
   NONFICTION / Social Topics / Civil & Human Rights | JUVENILE NONFICTION
   / People & Places / United States / African American & Black
Classification: LCC E185.615 .L4724 2023 (print) | LCC E185.615 (ebook) |
   DDC 323.1196/073—dc23/eng/20220823
LC record available at https://lccn.loc.gov/2022039916
LC ebook record available at https://lccn.loc.gov/2022039917

10 9 8 7 6 5 4 3 2 1   23 24 25 26 27

Printed in China   62
First edition, 2023

Composition by Kay Petronio

COVER & TITLE PAGE:
Justice Thurgood Marshall
on the steps of the Supreme
Court with his family on
September 1, 1967.

Millions of American soldiers fought in the Vietnam War, page 21.

Table of Contents

Dr. Martin Luther King, Jr., page 74.

African American workers sell fruits and vegetables in Virginia.

The Way It Was

The year 1865 was an important one in U.S. history. The American Civil War (1861–1865) ended and the Thirteenth **Amendment** to the U.S. Constitution was passed, **abolishing** slavery. This period of time also introduced Black codes in the form of **Jim Crow** laws. These laws restricted where people of color could live and work and were especially strict in the American South.

Jim Crow laws enforced **segregation**. Under the racial policy of "separate but equal," Black Americans could be given access to separate facilities if their quality was equal to that of white facilities. In reality, however, there was no equality. African Americans were forced to attend separate and inadequate schools and live in run-down neighborhoods.

The Fight Begins

As Jim Crow practices continued, two prominent **civil rights** organizations emerged. The National Association of Colored Women's Clubs (NACWC) was founded in 1896 by a group of politically active women, including Harriet Tubman. Members of the association dedicated themselves to fighting for voting rights and for ending racial violence in the form of **lynchings** against African Americans.

The National Association for the Advancement of Colored People (NAACP), founded in 1909, followed in the NACWC's footsteps. The NAACP focused on opposing segregation and Jim Crow policies. Both organizations would be crucial in the coming fight for justice.

Lasting Changes

In the following years, the Great Depression (1929–1939) and World War II (1939–1945) left Black Americans fighting for their lives at home and overseas. The 1954 U.S. Supreme Court decision in the *Brown v. Board of Education of Topeka* case challenging school segregation finally put an end to "separate but equal" in public schools. The years between 1955 and 1965 would serve as the heart of the civil rights movement. Rosa Parks refused to give up her seat on a bus, sparking the Montgomery bus **boycott**. The Reverend Dr. Martin Luther King, Jr., emerged as a leader and organized the March on Washington for Jobs and Freedom, the largest civil rights demonstration at the time.

The 1960s and 1970s further ignited those yearning for equal opportunities under the law. **Activists** continued to persevere, resulting in lasting changes for the African American community.

1967

The year 1967 was one of constant change in the United States. In this book, learn how President Lyndon B. Johnson sent thousands of African American soldiers to fight and die in the Vietnam War (1954–1975). Read about how civil rights leaders, including Dr. King, demanded peace. Discover how King organized the Poor People's Campaign to push for **economic** justice, and how racial inequality ignited riots across the country during what became known as the Long, Hot Summer of '67. Read about the triumphant day that Thurgood Marshall became the first African American Supreme Court justice. And find out how the Supreme Court case *Loving v. Virginia* finally allowed people of different racial backgrounds to marry each other legally and without fear. ■

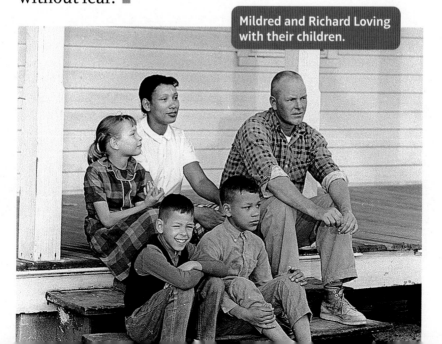

Mildred and Richard Loving with their children.

Edward Brooke was the first African American elected to the U.S. Senate from Massachusetts.

1

One Step Forward

On January 10, 1967, Edward W. Brooke made history when he strode proudly into the United States Senate. As he took his seat, the other senators leaped to their feet with applause: Senator Brooke of Massachusetts was the first African American elected to the position in the 20th century.

This wasn't his first time breaking racial barriers. In 1962, he became the first African American ever to serve as a state **attorney general**. Brooke served two terms in Massachusetts before running for Congress.

During his time in the Senate, he focused on housing inequality. Every American has the right to proper housing, but white Americans often barred African Americans from living in decent neighborhoods. Brooke promised to "unite men who have not been united before." Unfortunately, not every American was eager to bring diverse new voices into the U.S. government. On January 11, just one day after Brooke took his seat, Lester Maddox was sworn in as the 75th governor of Georgia.

Maddox, a white man, openly supported segregation. He insisted that white Americans and Black Americans should remain separate and unequal. He was also a violent man: In 1964, he'd threatened to shoot three young Black men just for entering his restaurant in Atlanta. In fact, when the **federal** government ordered him to allow Black customers in 1965, he closed his restaurant instead and ran for governor of Georgia.

Human Be-In

On January 14, 1967, more than 20,000 young protesters flooded into San Francisco's Golden Gate Park for the first-ever "Human Be-In." The Be-In took its name from the African American **sit-in** protests that had been happening across the country. These protests were especially popular in the South. During sit-ins, activists entered segregated establishments, such as restaurants and theaters, sat down, and refused to leave until the establishment agreed to serve them—their way of forcing the business to **integrate**. The tactic was extremely effective.

The Be-In was a peaceful demonstration. Thousands of activists came together in the park

An activist blows a giant bubble at Golden Gate Park in San Francisco.

to sing songs; pass around flowers, feathers, and candles; and play flutes and chimes. Artists gave speeches, and rock bands performed. Many of those in attendance were students.

The Be-In brought together diverse activists from many different causes. African American civil rights activists called for fair treatment and equal opportunities. Women's rights activists wanted better health-care options and gender equality in the workforce. And anti-war activists demanded that the government end the costly Vietnam War.

The Be-In proved that alone, each movement was strong, but united, they were unstoppable. Together, they could gain more national attention and win popular support. Together, they could transform the country.

A Strike at San Quentin

While protesters at the San Francisco Be-In demonstrated for racial equality, protesters just a few miles away in the same city were punished for it. On January 16, 1967, at San Quentin State Prison, 1,200 imprisoned African American men refused to work. The guards made them work more like animals than people, and they were exhausted. The imprisoned African American men began to strike, asking for better working conditions and fairer treatment.

The men protested peacefully for three days. After the strike ended, the guards took matters into their own hands. One guard deliberately provoked a small group of African American and white prisoners into

Imprisoned men in San Quentin State Prison faced terrible working conditions.

fighting one another. Soon, more men joined in. The fighting grew until several thousand men had come to blows.

When speaking to journalists about the strike, San Quentin officials claimed that it was a "race riot." This allowed them to distract the public from the real issues at the heart of the prison: **racism** and abuse. By dismissing the protests as a race riot, officials could act as if all imprisoned men—especially Black ones—were violent, needed to be controlled, and deserved to be in jail. San Quentin officials ignored Black protesters' actual concerns about **discrimination**. Instead, they played into white fears and **stereotypes** about Black violence.

No Justice in Mississippi

On February 28, 1967, three grieving families held their breath to see whether justice would be served. After the charges had been dismissed twice, 18 white men were **indicted** again for murdering three civil rights activists in 1964.

The activists had been volunteering with the Congress of Racial Equality (CORE) and the Freedom Summer campaign. They were registering Black voters in southern towns where African Americans were historically denied the right to vote. A group of 18 white men, infuriated by the campaign, kidnapped the

three activists, killed them, and buried them. Two of the activists, Michael Schwerner and Andrew Goodman, were white; the third, James Chaney, was Black.

The state of Mississippi wanted to let all 18 men go free, so the U.S. government had to step in and take the men to court. However, instead of charging the men with murder, the United States charged them with much lesser crimes: civil rights violations. Of the 18 indicted, only seven were found guilty of a violation, and they were all given minor sentences.

Ali Opposes the War

On March 6, legendary boxer Muhammad Ali learned that he would have to serve in the Vietnam War.

Freedom Summer

From June to August 1964, 700 volunteers traveled to
Mississippi, a southern state with harsh policies barring
African Americans from voting. In 1964, less than
7 percent of the Black population was registered to
vote. That's because city officials, police, and the
Ku Klux Klan (KKK) worked together to prevent African
Americans from even registering, much less casting
a ballot. The volunteers successfully registered 1,200
people in a single summer.

Freedom Summer
volunteers plan their
next demonstration.

Ali, who had been born Cassius Clay, was considered the greatest heavyweight champion of all time. As an African American athlete, he'd contended with racism both in and out of the boxing ring. He would one day become the first boxer to win the world heavyweight championship three separate times.

But as a member of the **Nation of Islam**, Ali opposed all types of war. When the U.S. military drafted him, he appealed three times; he asked them to release him from the draft because of his faith. On March 6, the military rejected his final appeal and ordered Ali to report to the army in April. Little did they know Ali would not go. ■

Muhammad Ali prepares for a boxing match in New York City.

Nation of Islam

Founded in 1930, the Nation of Islam is a religious and political organization that combines Islamic teachings with ideas about Black pride. During the 1960s, the Nation called for all African Americans to unify in the protest for civil rights. The Nation also encouraged its members to change their names, because many African Americans' last names reflected the families who had enslaved their ancestors. The most famous member was civil rights leader Malcolm X.

Civil rights activist Malcolm X delivers a speech at an outdoor rally.

With Dr. King at his side, President Johnson (seated) signs the Civil Rights Act of 1964.

2

Beyond Vietnam

Dr. King was famous for his commitment to peace. However, he often remained silent on one issue: the Vietnam War. Even though the war had killed thousands of American soldiers, Vietnamese soldiers, and Vietnamese **civilians**, King had never organized a public demonstration against it. That changed on March 25, 1967, when he led his first march in protest of the Vietnam War. He and 5,000 anti-war demonstrators marched through the city of Chicago, Illinois.

The war had begun 13 years earlier, in 1954. There was a reason King had been silent for so long. He wanted the president, Lyndon B. Johnson, to pass key civil rights **legislation**, such as the Civil Rights Act of 1964 and the Voting Rights Act of 1965. King knew that publicly opposing Johnson's decisions in Vietnam would only have a negative impact on his relationship with the president and would therefore make Johnson hesitant to work with him.

But now, with movements like the Human Be-In attracting tens of thousands of protesters as the anti-war movement swelled across the country, King had to do something. The greater American public was turning against the war. He had to help make sure their voices were heard.

The Vietnam War

The Vietnam War was a costly and complicated one. The United States supported South Vietnam, which was fighting against **Communist** North Vietnam. In the 1960s, the United States sent a flood of armed American troops into South Vietnam.

The war escalated year after year. President Johnson shipped 185,000 troops to Vietnam in 1965. By the end of 1966, there were more than 400,000 stationed there. To meet the demand for soldiers, the U.S. government **drafted** hundreds of thousands of young men ages 18 to 26, forcing them to join the military.

Vietnam was the first U.S. war in which Black and white Americans fought side by side instead of in segregated units. Unfortunately, African Americans still faced heavy discrimination from their fellow soldiers. They were rarely promoted to be officers. They were also more likely than white soldiers to be assigned to dangerous combat units with a higher risk of death; 45 to 60 percent of dangerous airborne units were made up entirely of Black men. In the United States, some southern communities refused to bury fallen Black soldiers in unsegregated cemeteries.

By the end of the Vietnam War in 1975, more than three million people would be killed. Of them, 58,000 were Americans. More than 1.5 million were innocent Vietnamese civilians who had nothing to do with the fighting. In the end, the United States and South Vietnam lost the war.

2.7 million Americans fought in the Vietnam War.

Wounded American soldiers walk to a field hospital in Vietnam.

Project 100,000

Compared to their white counterparts, young African American men were more likely to be drafted into the Vietnam War and, in the case of Project 100,000, more likely to die there. In 1967, African Americans made up 11 percent of the U.S. population but comprised 16.3 percent of men drafted. The same year, the military drafted 64 percent of eligible African Americans, but only 31 percent of eligible white Americans.

Worse still was the military's controversial campaign called Project 100,000. As part of this project, which started in 1966, the military drafted men who didn't meet their usual educational and medical requirements. Many of these men had intellectual disabilities.

After this project began, African Americans began getting drafted at increasingly higher rates. Of the project's 246,000 draftees, 40 percent were Black. Soldiers in Project 100,000 died at higher rates than other soldiers. The total number of U.S. troops in Vietnam more than doubled between 1965 and 1967. In total, 300,000 African Americans would serve in the war, and 7,262 would die.

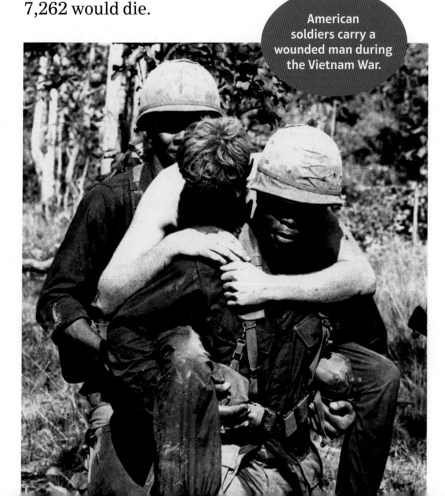

American soldiers carry a wounded man during the Vietnam War.

A Controversial Speech

As the draft tore apart countless Black communities, Dr. King further recognized the evils of the Vietnam War. On April 4, 1967, King delivered the most iconic anti-war speech of his career: "Beyond Vietnam."

Three thousand spectators gathered at Riverside Church in New York City to hear him speak. In the speech, he pointed out all the ways in which the Vietnam War was severely holding back the civil rights movement.

For starters, the United States was spending increasingly more money on the military and increasingly less on social programs to help end poverty and address unequal access to housing, health care, and education. In other words, military spending was prohibiting economic equality.

King also pointed out that the war wasn't just affecting soldiers. It was killing innocent Vietnamese civilians, including women and children. He proposed a five-point plan. At the top of the list: a **cease-fire**. The United States would have to lay down its weapons.

This was King's most controversial speech. Longtime allies from the NAACP criticized him, claiming that by expanding his message to include

Dr. King delivers his "Beyond Vietnam" speech at Riverside Church.

the Vietnam War, he was distracting from the core goal—achieving Black civil rights. Major newspapers such as the *New York Times* and the *Washington Post* called the speech a mistake.

King lost white support as well. Public figures who had once stood beside him, such as President Johnson, now distanced themselves. It was one thing to support King's message of peace, unity, and brotherhood in the United States. It was another to support it in Vietnam. Many Americans weren't willing to do that.

Spring Mobilization Committee Begins

Despite the initial public backlash against Dr. King, it became increasingly clear that the anti-war movement was gaining steam. On April 15, 1967, 100,000 people from an anti-war organization called the Spring Mobilization Committee to End the War in Vietnam (Mobe) marched in San Francisco. That was a crowd five times larger than that of the Be-In that had taken place just a few months earlier. They packed an entire stadium.

On the same day, in New York City, the Mobe led a protest of 125,000 demonstrators. They marched from Central Park to the headquarters of the United Nations. African American

100,000 peace demonstrators march through San Francisco.

Dr. King (center) leads an anti-war protest in New York City.

activist James Bevel headed the committee as its national director. Bevel was a leader in the Southern Christian Leadership Conference (SCLC), one of the most powerful civil rights organizations in the country, and he had a close relationship with King. By also heading the Spring Mobilization Committee, Bevel signaled that ending the war was necessary to achieve civil rights.

King led the march alongside Bevel. During the event, Bevel got swept up in the moment and made a spontaneous announcement: The Mobe would hold another anti-war gathering in Washington, DC. This gathering would be called the Spring Mobilization Conference. Although Bevel didn't know it yet, the Washington gathering would raise the anti-war movement to new heights. ∎

Muhammad Ali discusses his refusal to fight in the Vietnam War.

3

The Summer of
Loving v. Virginia

Dr. King's "Beyond Vietnam" speech lit a spark in the anti-war movement, and the Spring Mobilization Committee's New York march fanned the flame. The movement surged in popularity as more Americans began to speak out against the war—and more and more celebrities did, too.

On April 28, 1967, the now world-famous boxer Muhammad Ali made it clear that he didn't just oppose the war. He publicly refused to fight, even though he had been drafted, because it contradicted his religious beliefs as a member of the Nation of Islam. Because refusing the draft was a federal crime, the U.S. government sentenced him to prison for five years and fined him $10,000. But the punishment didn't stop there.

The New York State Athletic Commission and the World Boxing Association also stripped Ali of his championship boxing titles. On top of that, they banned him from professional boxing for three years. For the 25-year-old Ali, three years was a lifetime. He was now in his prime physically and would find it difficult to return to peak form after three years outside the ring.

Ali stuck to his beliefs. He stayed out of prison while his case was being **appealed**. The U.S. Supreme Court wouldn't overturn his conviction until 1971, when it acknowledged his right to refuse to serve due to religious beliefs.

The Black Panthers March Against Mulford

In 1967, most white politicians were eager to give African Americans guns and send them to die in the Vietnam War. But they didn't want African Americans carrying guns while they were living in the United States.

These white politicians were hypocritical about gun control laws. They believed that Americans should have the freedom to have guns—but only if they were white. This became all too clear on May 2, when members of the Black Panther Party calmly marched into the California State Capitol building holding guns. They didn't shoot; it was intended as a peaceful demonstration.

According to California law at the time, gun owners were allowed to carry their guns in public. Therefore, this march was completely legal. The Panthers were protesting the Mulford Act. This law would forbid people from carrying loaded guns in public, and it targeted the Black Panthers, who carried guns to protect themselves while doing safety patrols through their Oakland neighborhoods. During these safety patrols, heavily armed police often harassed and threatened them, so the Panthers carried the guns for their own safety. If the police were allowed to wield weapons and the Panthers weren't, the Panthers would be vulnerable to attacks. So they marched into the Capitol in protest.

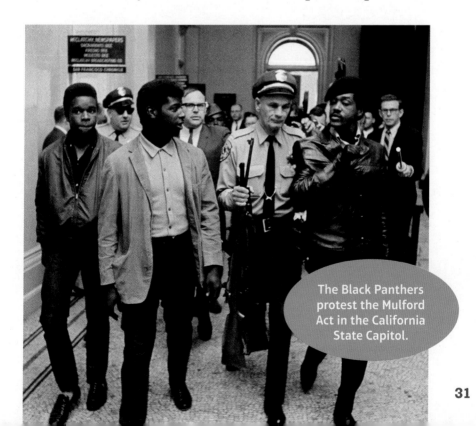

The Black Panthers protest the Mulford Act in the California State Capitol.

Black Panther Party

The Black Panther Party was founded by Black activists Bobby Seale and Huey P. Newton in October 1966 in Oakland, California. This civil rights organization stood for Black Nationalism—the desire to form a separate and independent nation of their own—and fought against police brutality in particular. The group also started social programs, such as providing free breakfast to local children and opening community health clinics.

Huey Newton (right) and Bobby Seale led the Black Panthers.

"THE RACIST DOG POLICEMEN MUST WITHDRAW IMMEDIATELY FROM OUR COMMUNITIES, CEASE THEIR WANTON MURDER AND BRUTALITY AND TORTURE OF BLACK PEOPLE, OR FACE THE WRATH OF THE ARMED PEOPLE."

HUEY P. NEWTON, Minister of Defense

BLACK PANTHER PARTY
P.O. Box 8641, Emeryville, Calif.

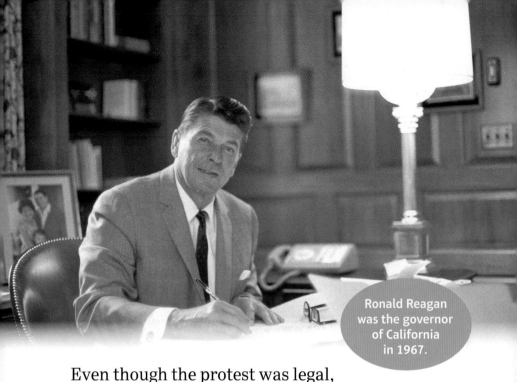

Ronald Reagan was the governor of California in 1967.

Even though the protest was legal, white Americans grew alarmed. Politicians scrambled to pass new laws that would closely restrict what people could do with their firearms. Ronald Reagan, who would be elected president in 1980, was one of those politicians. As the governor of California at the time, he hurried to sign the Mulford Act.

Spring Mobilization Conference

During the Spring Mobilization Committee's New York City march, James Bevel had promised to hold an even larger conference in Washington, DC. That conference took place on May 20 and 21. Hundreds of anti-war activists gathered to plan the next steps for the peace movement. The movement was gaining steam, and it needed a grand strategy.

The Mobe agreed to organize protests every month, and it decided to hold the largest protest in October 1967. It would become one of the most massive anti-war demonstrations that the United States had ever seen.

Summer of Love

In the summer of 1967, love was in the air in San Francisco, California. January's Human Be-In inspired a transformative new movement; in early June of that year, about 75,000 young anti-war activists flowed into the city from all over the country. They represented many different ethnic, social, and religious backgrounds, but they all had one goal: peace.

The young activists called for civil rights, women's rights, and an end to the Vietnam War. The protesters all lived together in harmony, sharing everything they had, and spent days creating art.

A band plays at Golden Gate Park in San Francisco.

Dr. David Smith (left) with two volunteers at the Haight Ashbury Free Medical Clinic.

Haight Ashbury Free Medical Clinic

Just a few days into the Summer of Love, it became clear that the protesters might need health care. On June 7, Dr. David E. Smith opened the Haight Ashbury Free Medical Clinic, which provided free medical care to anyone in need. It started as a temporary project that would serve a single neighborhood in San Francisco, the neighborhood of Haight-Ashbury. But its popularity boomed.

Soon, free clinics popped up around the country. Five more would open by the end of the year. By 1970, 75 free clinics were operating in the United States and Canada. Free clinics were in high demand because millions of low-income people across the country—not just young protesters—desperately needed affordable health care. The Black Panthers would join the free clinic movement, opening community health centers that offered care to African Americans who were denied treatment otherwise.

An activist changes a street sign during the Summer of Love.

This movement, which lasted for four months, was called the Summer of Love.

Loving v. Virginia

The protesters in San Francisco were not the only ones taking a positive stance on love in 1967. On June 12, the Supreme Court handed down a landmark decision that would change the face of marriage in America. The Court declared that African Americans and white Americans could legally marry all over the country. They declared that people of *all* races should be able to exercise this right.

This decision was thanks to two brave people who didn't let fear stop them from loving each other: Mildred and Richard Loving. Mildred, a woman of color, and Richard, a white man, had been sentenced to a year in prison for entering Virginia as a married couple. The Lovings both grew up in Virginia, where the Virginia Racial Integrity Act of 1924 banned people of different races from marrying each other, because their children would ruin the "integrity" (or the so-called purity) of the white race.

In Virginia, interracial marriage was a **felony**, and anyone caught engaging in it could be sent to prison for up to 25 years. Virginia wasn't the only state to enforce such a law. In fact, in 1967, 15 other states mainly in the South banned interracial marriage.

Mr. and Mrs. Loving took their case to the Supreme Court.

The Lovings knew this, but they were high school sweethearts who wanted to marry each other, no matter how difficult it would be. They agreed the risk was worth it. They got married in Washington, DC, where interracial marriage was legal. Just five weeks after they returned to Virginia, the police arrested them. It didn't matter that they'd gotten married in a place where it was legal: In the eyes of Virginia law, their marriage was still illegal.

The courts in Virginia found them guilty and offered the Lovings a choice: They could leave the state for 25 years, abandoning their friends, their family, their careers, and the only home they'd ever known. Or they could go to prison.

The Lovings took their case to the Virginia Supreme Court, but that court sided with the Virginia law.

Next, the Lovings took their case to the U.S. Supreme Court. Their lawyer argued that the Virginia Act should be illegal because it violated the Fourteenth Amendment, which promised all citizens equal protection under the law. The Supreme Court unanimously agreed with the Lovings—any laws banning interracial marriage were discriminatory, and therefore had to be abolished. The Court immediately declared interracial marriage

No. 420276   **Marriage License**

To Reverend ____John L. Henry_____

authorized to celebrate marriages in the District of Columbia, GREETING:

You are hereby authorized to celebrate the rites of marriage between

_____Richard Perry Loving_____, of ____Passing, Virginia____

AND

_____Mildred Delores Jeter_____, of ____Passing, Virginia____

and having done so, you are commanded to make return of the same to the Clerk's Office of the United States District Court for the District of Columbia within TEN days, under a penalty of $50 for default therein.

WITNESS my hand and seal of said Court, this___2nd_____

day of_____June_____, anno Domini 19 58_

HARRY M. HULL, Clerk.

By ____Maud R Rynex_____

Deputy Clerk

No. 420276   **Return**

I, Reverend_____John L. Henry_____

who have been duly authorized to celebrate the rites of marriage in the District of Columbia, do hereby certify that, by authority of license of corresponding number herewith, I solemnized the marriage of_____

_____Richard Perry Loving_____ and ____Mildred Delores Jeter_____

named therein, on the__2nd__day of___June_____, 19_58_, at __748 Princeton Place, N. W.__

in said District.   (Name of church, or street address, etc.)

6/4/58   ewg

FPI ERO—6-19-57-10M-7208   ____Rev. John L. Henry_____

An image of Richard and Mildred Loving's marriage license from 1958.

legal throughout the country. The Lovings, who had moved to Washington, DC, could return to Virginia.

This was a huge victory! It was a victory not only for the Lovings, but for all interracial couples who had been living in fear. Unfortunately, not every state complied with the Supreme Court's decision. Several states kept their laws banning interracial marriage, even though the federal government had prohibited states from enforcing such laws.

Alabama was the last state to make a legal change. It didn't remove its law against interracial marriage from the state constitution until 2000— 33 years after the *Loving v. Virginia* decision. ∎

Smoke pours out of a building during the "race riot" in Detroit.

4

The Long, Hot Summer of '67

For San Francisco's peace activists, the Summer of Love promised optimism, hope, and harmony. But for African Americans, that summer meant something entirely different: It was the Long, Hot Summer of '67.

That summer, one intense and powerful demonstration after another broke out across the country as African Americans protested racism, discrimination, police brutality, and unfair treatment. In total, there would be 159 protests. Newspapers called them violent "race riots," ignoring the complex histories and causes behind the demonstrations.

Newark Rebellion

One of the most significant demonstrations was the Newark Rebellion, which took place from July 12 to July 17. Many Black Americans had moved to northern cities such as Newark, New Jersey, decades earlier during the Great Migration (1910–1970), hoping to escape the segregation of the Jim Crow South. However, in many cases, they were still treated as second-class citizens in the North.

In Newark, Black Americans endured housing and job discrimination that pushed them into poverty. On top of that, they were routinely locked out of politics and suffered at the hands of the police. On July 12, two white police officers beat a Black cab driver. African

American residents of Newark rallied in protest. The protest lasted five days. The city called in police officers and the National Guard, who arrested 1,465 people. There were more than 700 injuries and 26 deaths.

On July 17, similar protests began in Cairo, Illinois, after a Black soldier was found dead in a jail cell. On July 19, protests spread to Minneapolis, Minnesota, and Durham, North Carolina; protests in Memphis, Tennessee, began on July 20.

Detroit Uprising

On July 23, 1967, the bloodiest protest of the summer began: the Detroit Rebellion, also known as the Detroit Uprising.

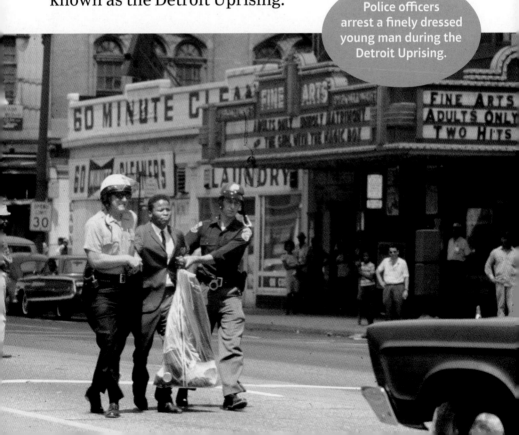

Police officers arrest a finely dressed young man during the Detroit Uprising.

Shops were broken into during the Detroit Uprising.

Detroit was no stranger to protests. In 1943, African Americans who'd moved to the mostly white area protested employment discrimination, harsh policing, and a lack of affordable housing. The 1943 protests became violent. Although Black people had been the *victims*, not the perpetrators, of most of the violence, the police and the press still blamed them for the "race riot."

By 1967, not much had improved in Detroit: 93 percent of the police force was white, although the population was 30 percent Black, and Black residents faced constant police brutality. Black residents often asked the city for police reform, but their requests were ignored.

Black people were forced to take low-paying, menial jobs—that is, when they were employed at all. In the 1950s, 15.9 percent of Black Americans were unemployed nationwide, compared to 6 percent of white Americans. Black Americans were also commonly denied bank loans and decent housing. Unable to live in good neighborhoods, Black families had to send their children to underfunded public schools as well. Black children with poor education therefore found it even harder to get jobs as adults. The cycle of poverty continued.

Many Black Americans faced discrimination at white-owned bars and restaurants.

Jerome Cavanagh

Jerome Cavanagh was mayor of Detroit from 1962 to 1970. While campaigning, he promised African Americans that he would bring social change. At first, he did. He started an **affirmative action** program to help the city employ more minorities. He marched with Dr. King in the 1963 Detroit Walk to Freedom. However, although he appeared to push for small changes on the surface, he did not do enough to address the underlying **systemic** discrimination that left many African American Detroiters dissatisfied. This led to the Detroit Rebellion. He did not run for reelection after his second term ended.

Jerome Cavanagh served as the mayor of Detroit.

The Detroit Uprising began at a blind pig, the name for after-hours bars.

Even establishments that claimed to be integrated and open to people of all races treated their non-white customers poorly. Tired of the mistreatment, Black Americans opened their own restaurants and clubs.

The police raided these Black-owned businesses often. On July 23, 1967, Detroit police stormed an after-hours bar. At the time, the 82 people inside were celebrating the safe return of two Black soldiers from the Vietnam War. Police arrested everyone present.

This was the last straw. Outraged and exhausted, nearby Black residents protested. The protests spread like wildfire through Detroit.

On July 25, U.S. Army troops, authorized by President Johnson, marched into Detroit. Over the next several days, 8,500 members of the Michigan National Guard and 800 Michigan State Police also turned violently against the protesters. Soldiers used tanks and machine guns on civilians. One guardsman, Sergeant Mortimer LeBlanc, fired into an apartment, killing a four-year-old girl. He was cleared of all charges.

The police abused both Black and white Detroiters whom they took into custody. As violence increased, the Michigan Civil Rights Commission attempted to defend the rights of people being arrested, but they were limited in what they could do.

The rebellion lasted until July 28. Ultimately, the civilian protesters were no match for Johnson's federal troops. The troops had an arsenal of military machinery at the ready and were prepared to attack

The National Guard fills the streets of Detroit.

with the full strength of the U.S. military—even when facing unarmed civilians.

In total, 43 people died: 33 Black people and 10 white people. Of the 7,200 people arrested, the majority were Black. Houses were also destroyed during the demonstrations, leaving 5,000 people homeless. This was the most intense uprising the United States had experienced in more than a century.

Kerner Commission

President Johnson wanted to know what caused the Detroit Rebellion, perhaps understanding that Detroit's unrest would help shed light on the reasons

Otto Kerner headed the National Advisory Committee on Civil Disorders following the Long, Hot Summer of '67.

behind the other 158 protests of the Long, Hot Summer of '67.

On July 28, before troops had even left Detroit's streets, Johnson created the National Advisory Commission on Civil Disorders to research and determine what had led to the Detroit Rebellion. Because the commission was led by Illinois Governor Otto Kerner, Jr., it became known as the Kerner Commission.

In the White House, President Johnson (seated, left) meets with the National Advisory Committee on Civil Disorders.

The Commission's findings were crystal clear. In the document, they confirmed what city officials already knew and what activists had been saying for a long time: African Americans were protesting because they were denied economic opportunities, and because they were sick of unrelenting discrimination and police brutality.

The Kerner Report offered a solution that was more like a warning. The U.S. government needed to provide better public services and housing programs to correct the centuries of job, education, and housing discrimination that had historically kept African Americans impoverished.

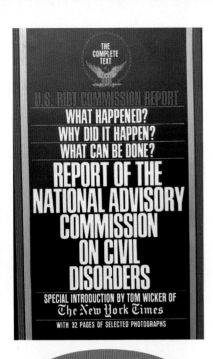

THE COMPLETE TEXT

U.S. RIOT COMMISSION REPORT
WHAT HAPPENED?
WHY DID IT HAPPEN?
WHAT CAN BE DONE?
REPORT OF THE NATIONAL ADVISORY COMMISSION ON CIVIL DISORDERS
SPECIAL INTRODUCTION BY TOM WICKER OF
The New York Times
WITH 32 PAGES OF SELECTED PHOTOGRAPHS

A report revealed the root causes of the Long, Hot Summer of '67.

Johnson suppressed the report, trying to keep the general public from rallying around its findings. But the 708-page published report became a best-selling book.

Aftermath of the Detroit Rebellion

Johnson couldn't suppress the report, and he couldn't stop the consequences of the Detroit Rebellion. As a result of the protests, white residents left Detroit in large numbers. This "white flight," as it was called, had been happening across the country, but the protests sped up the process. Between 1967 and 1969, most of the 173,000 white residents left Detroit, and Detroit's public schools lost 74 percent of their white students between 1967 and 1978.

Meanwhile, minority hiring within state and local governments increased, and on August 18, 1967, the Michigan State Police Department swore in the state's first Black trooper. In 1968, 35 percent of police hired were Black, and fair housing opportunities increased steadily in the city. ◼

Great Migration and White Flight

From 1910 to 1970, African Americans moved in large numbers from the South to the North looking for better job opportunities and an escape from Jim Crow segregation. This movement became known as the Great Migration. During the 1950s and 1960s, in response to integration, middle-class white families began to move out of these increasingly diverse areas and into all-white suburbs, where pricing and zoning regulations kept minorities from purchasing homes. This was called "white flight."

White suburban neighborhoods like this one in Levittown, NY, sprang up as a result of white flight.

Thurgood Marshall became the first African American Supreme Court justice.

5

Thurgood Marshall: A Supreme Decision

Not long after the Supreme Court struck down interracial marriage laws throughout the country, the Court made another historic step toward equality. On August 30, Thurgood Marshall was officially confirmed as the first African American Supreme Court justice in American history.

For Marshall, born in 1908, this was the culmination of a lifetime of hard work. As a Black man in the American South, Marshall had to fight for everything he had in life. He graduated with honors from Lincoln University in Pennsylvania in 1930 with aspirations of becoming a lawyer.

Walter E. Washington

Thurgood Marshall wasn't the only one making history in the American capital that autumn. On September 6, 1967, President Johnson appointed Walter E. Washington as mayor of Washington, DC. Washington became the first African American mayor of any major American city. Like Thurgood Marshall, Washington was descended from slaves and graduated from Howard University School of Law. Until Washington's appointment, DC had not had a mayor for 96 years, since 1871. Washington would serve for more than a decade, until 1979.

Walter E. Washington is sworn in as the mayor of Washington, DC.

He dreamed of going to the **prestigious** University of Maryland School of Law. However, although his grades were good enough, the school rejected him simply because he was Black.

Murray v. Pearson

Marshall didn't let this keep him from becoming a lawyer. Instead, he attended Howard University School of Law, a historically Black institution. He graduated first in his class in 1933.

Among his first legal victories, one hit very close to home. The case was *Murray v. Pearson* in 1935. A young Black man had been denied admission to the University of Maryland School of Law—which Marshall had once dreamed of attending—because of his race.

The 1896 *Plessy v. Ferguson* case had declared that institutions for Black and white Americans had to be "separate but equal." However, in the Maryland Court of Appeals, Marshall argued that in Maryland, these institutions

Baltimore Boy Finishes Law

Thurgood Marshall, of Baltimore, was the only honor graduate of the Howard University Law School for the year 1933 being cum laude. gradu a t e d. He was one of the eight out of the sixteen students of the class of 1933 who were graduated Friday at the school commencement. Mr. Marshall is graduate of Lincoln University, the son of Mr. and Mrs. Wm. Marshall, and attended the Douglass High School of this city. His brother, Dr. W. Aubrey Marshall, is a practising physician here.

⁒ **Thurgood Marshall**

Marshall graduated with honors from Howard University School of Law.

Marshall (left) represents an African American man during *Murray v. Pearson*.

were not equal. White institutions were always superior. Therefore, they should not be separate.

Marshall won this case, forcing the university to integrate. During his argument, Marshall referenced the Fourteenth Amendment, stating that "separate but equal" violated the equal protection clause—the right for every American to be equally protected by the law and by the government.

In 1936, Marshall began working with and representing the NAACP, taking civil rights court cases. The Fourteenth Amendment clause would become the backbone for future civil rights cases, including *Loving v. Virginia*.

Chambers v. Florida

In 1940, Marshall founded a new, specialized division of the NAACP, the NAACP Legal Defense and Educational Fund. This allowed him to focus on bringing cases to court—not just to the Maryland Court of Appeals, like *Murray v. Pearson,* but to the Supreme Court itself.

That year, Marshall argued his first case before the Supreme Court: *Chambers v. Florida.* Police had arrested four Black men for the death of a white man. The officers had denied the Black men their right to legal representation,

Marshall (left) and the NAACP Legal Defense Fund staff in 1960.

held them for a week without charges, and eventually intimidated them into confessing. Such police tactics were common. Police often arrested African Americans without cause and tortured them until they signed false confessions for crimes they didn't commit.

In this groundbreaking case, Marshall argued that this practice was **unconstitutional**. Forced confessions should not count as evidence, because people being tortured would confess anything the police wanted to hear, whether or not it was true. Marshall won. This case forbade police officers from forcing confessions out of the people they arrested.

Chambers v. Florida was a landmark case, but the biggest case of Marshall's career as a lawyer, by far, was *Brown v. Board of Education of Topeka* in 1954, which combated segregation in U.S. public schools.

Newspapers report the end of segregation in U.S. public schools.

Brown v. Board

In 1954, Thurgood Marshall dealt a major blow to the segregationist movement with the case *Brown v. Board of Education of Topeka*. In the case, an African American man sued the Topeka, Kansas, Board of Education after his daughter was denied entrance to an all-white school in Topeka. Marshall argued successfully that "separate but equal" was a lie, since schools for Black children were, by design, categorically worse than schools for white children. Therefore, all public schools must be integrated. The Supreme Court justices ruled unanimously in his favor.

On paper, Marshall's win essentially ended segregation in public schools in the United States. For the first time in American history, Black and white children everywhere would learn side by side, equally. However, many states still refused to integrate. In some cases, police and federal troops had to step in to physically protect African American students from angry mobs as they tried to enter all-white schools.

In response to integration, many white families engaged in white flight, moving their children out of diverse areas and into all-white suburbs.

Marshall (center) celebrates on May 17, 1954, right after school segregation is ruled unconstitutional.

In total, Marshall won 29 out of the 32 cases he took to the Supreme Court.

Other notable cases included *Shelley v. Kraemer* (1948), a ruling about housing **covenants**. A housing covenant was a document that listed who could or could not own a certain property. Many covenants prohibited that property from ever being sold to African Americans or Asian Americans. Marshall persuaded the Supreme Court to make it illegal to enforce housing covenants based on race because that violated the Fourteenth Amendment.

He also won *McLaurin v. Oklahoma State Regents for*

During *Shelley v. Kraemer*, Marshall represented the Shelley family.

Higher Education (1950), forcing the Supreme Court to integrate all graduate and professional schools.

Marshall Joins the Court

In 1965, President Johnson appointed Thurgood Marshall as the first African American U.S. solicitor general. This made him the highest-ranking African American government official the United States had ever had. The solicitor general represents the United States in Supreme Court cases, arguing on behalf of the government. In his two-year run as solicitor general, Marshall won 14 out of 19 cases.

Once a seat on the Supreme Court opened up, Johnson nominated Marshall as a Supreme Court justice. The Senate confirmed him on August 30, 1967. On October 2, Marshall was sworn in.

Marshall takes his seat for the first time as a Supreme Court justice.

Thurgood Marshall served on the Supreme Court for 24 years. His legal philosophy was: "You do what you think is right and let the law catch up." That certainly described Marshall. Over the course of his career, he continually broke down barriers and worked to undo centuries of discrimination.

He helped decide the case *Furman v. Georgia* (1972), which declared that the death penalty, which was given to Black Americans more often than white Americans, was illegal. This temporarily banned the death penalty in the United States. When members of the Supreme Court moved to allow the death penalty again after the case *Gregg v. Georgia* (1976), Marshall strongly opposed it.

He also stood for women's rights. He ruled in favor of *Roe v. Wade* (1973), giving women access to important health-care services. In *Personnel Administrator of Massachusetts v. Feeney* (1979), he argued that it was unconstitutional to give hiring preferences to veterans over non-veterans, because most veterans were men, and this would negatively affect women.

A newspaper declares the death penalty is illegal in 1972.

Marshall retired in 1991. Clarence Thomas, another African American judge, replaced him and is currently the longest-serving member of the Court. ■

Clarence Thomas is sworn in as a Supreme Court justice.

THIS IS NOT A PUBLIC ENTRANCE. AD-
MITTANCE PERMITTED TO SELECTIVE
SERVICE REGISTRANTS ORDERED TO
REPORT BY THE LOCAL BOARDS. AP-
PLICANTS REFERRED BY THE RECRUIT-
ING SERVICES. PERSONNEL ASSIGNED
TO, OR EMPLOYED BY THE AFEES.
ALL OTHERS USE THE 1515 CLAY
STREET ENTRANCE.

VE COME IN PEACE

Activists protest the Vietnam War at the Oakland Army Induction Center.

6

Stop the War, Help the Poor

Within its own borders, the United States was taking steps toward justice and racial equality. But overseas, the Vietnam War raged on, and Americans were becoming increasingly dissatisfied. During October 16–20, 1967, in the week leading up to the National Mobilization Committee protest that James Bevel had promised in the spring, thousands of protesters gathered in the Bay Area of California for Stop the Draft Week.

Stop the Draft Week

The week began with 300 men mailing their draft cards back to the U.S. government, a form of protest called "turning in" draft cards. Another popular method of getting rid of draft cards was to burn them. Anyone who burned a draft card,

Police officers hold back peaceful demonstrators in Oakland, CA.

even if that person wasn't registered for the draft, could be arrested.

Not content to simply protest by mail, 3,000 activists gathered in front of the Oakland Army Induction Center on the same day. The center was the administrative building where military officials processed draftees.

The 3,000 protesters peacefully handed out anti-war leaflets to the soldiers who had just been inducted, urging them to change their minds and refuse induction. The next day, police came to meet the protesters. As protesters peacefully marched and sang, officers attacked them with clubs, boots, and tear gas.

Despite the risk of police violence, protesters returned the next day, and the next. Each day, their numbers grew bigger. By the end of the week, there were more than 10,000.

March in Washington

On October 21, 1967, one of the most significant demonstrations against the Vietnam War took place in Washington, DC.

Seventy thousand protesters marched at a rally at the Lincoln Memorial, a site that had seen countless civil rights demonstrations. The most notable one was the 1963 March on Washington for Jobs and Freedom, during which Dr. King had delivered his famous "I Have a Dream" speech, rallying hundreds of thousands of people to the civil rights movement. Now James Bevel, a close confidant of King, was heading the next phase of the civil rights movement. As long as the United States was at war, there would be no justice for African Americans.

During the 1967 Lincoln Memorial rally, famous poets, politicians, and doctors spoke about the importance of ending the war. Protesters carried signs, chanted, and sang.

When they had planned the protest in May, some members of the Mobe suggested that they storm the U.S. Capitol and occupy it. But Mobe leaders quickly

scrapped that idea because they didn't want to be another disruptive, violent political force. Instead, they came up with a different plan: March to the Pentagon, where the U.S. Department of Defense was located, and use their minds to make the building float 300 feet in the air.

Of course, activists didn't actually believe they could make the Pentagon float. But when speaking to the press, they pretended that they did. The press latched on to this crazy idea and spread it like wild-fire. For the Mobe, this was great advertising. Many people who heard about the floating Pentagon plans joined the march that day simply because they

Anti-war protestors gather at the Lincoln Memorial during the March on the Pentagon.

admired the activists' creativity. Others attended the march to see for themselves whether the Pentagon might leave the ground.

After the speech at the Lincoln Memorial, protesters marched to the Pentagon. There, military police and federal marshals were waiting, ready to herd them into special protest areas. The crowd was diverse, composed of Black activists, white **hippies**, middle-class professionals, and clergymen, among others. Organizers distributed anti-war leaflets throughout the crowd. A truck delivered 200 pounds of flowers, and activists passed them out to everyone gathered. Photographers took pictures of protesters gently placing daisies into the barrels of the military police's guns.

As a result of the protest, the general public began to view the Pentagon differently. For many Americans, the Department of Defense lost a lot of its authority. Images of protesters dancing, singing, and placing flowers into gun barrels sent the message that it was okay to question the government, because its authority was not absolute.

America's First Black Mayors

In 1967, Cleveland, Ohio, was the ninth-largest city in the United States, and 68 percent

A peaceful protestor puts a carnation in a soldier's gun.

white. So it came as a shock when, on November 7, Carl Stokes was voted mayor. This made him the first elected African American mayor of a major American city.

The same day, Richard Hatcher was elected the first African American mayor of Gary, Indiana. He would serve for 20 years. He and Stokes were the first African Americans to be elected mayors of U.S. cities with populations of more than 100,000 people.

Carl Stokes is sworn in as the mayor of Cleveland.

Poor People's Campaign

On November 27, 1967, Dr. King met with the SCLC. They needed to discuss their next steps as an organization. Over the previous decade, they had achieved countless victories. This included ending legal segregation and the passage of both the Civil Rights Act of 1964 and the Voting Rights Act of 1965. Now they had to tackle issues that were a bit more complex.

Making sure that African American children and white children could legally attend the same schools was one thing. But if African American families could never make as much money as white families, then they would never live in the same school zones. Plus, because schools were funded by taxes, white schools in wealthy districts would still be better funded than Black schools. These types of inequalities had led to the rebellions during the Long, Hot Summer of '67.

King had authored his own report about the Long, Hot Summer of '67, called "The Crisis in America's Cities." In this short document, King explained how American politicians had

Dr. King (left) stands with an archbishop outside the SCLC headquarters.

The Poor People's Campaign protested for economic justice.

purposefully created unequal economic conditions. "They created discrimination; they created slums; they perpetuate unemployment, ignorance and poverty," he wrote of the "policy makers of the white society."

It was clear: The civil rights movement must evolve to focus on economic inequality. King wanted to launch a new campaign for basic economic rights, such as a fair minimum wage and educational opportunities for adults as well as children.

The question was, how should this new campaign look? King didn't approve of rioting, but younger activists criticized his nonviolent approach for being weak and ineffective. King's new campaign would have to be like nothing he'd ever organized before.

Sly and the Integration of Music

A major staple of protests was music. As protesters from different cultural backgrounds came together in organizations like the Mobe, their musical styles blended together, too. October 1967 saw the release of Sly and the Family Stone's debut album, *A Whole New Thing*. This band was groundbreaking for two reasons: Not only was it the first major mixed-gender band, with men and women singing side by side, but it was also the first interracial band. Sly's multicultural music combined genres, blending funk, Motown pop, soul, **psychedelic** rock, and even Broadway show tunes, while singing about peace among all people.

Sly and the Family Stone made headlines as the first interracial band.

Senator Robert F. Kennedy, brother of the late President John F. Kennedy, asked activist Marian Wright Edelman to "tell Dr. King to bring the poor people to Washington to make hunger and poverty visible."

King decided to do just that. The following year, he planned to march thousands of impoverished Americans straight into the heart of Washington, DC, to confront politicians directly and to demand basic economic rights. This new movement would unite activists from African American, Indigenous, Puerto Rican, Mexican American, and poor white communities. The Poor People's Campaign was born.

King officially announced the campaign on December 4, stating that American society had to completely transform in order to fix its three evils: poverty, racism, and war. He called on the SCLC to expand its focus from civil rights for African Americans to human rights for all people, and to pivot from gradual reform to total revolution.

The Poor People's Campaign aimed to address poverty by focusing on income inequality, housing, and the creation of an Economic Bill of Rights. King demanded more low-income housing and a guaranteed annual income. The campaign would officially kick off in 1968.

Bobby Seale announces the Black Panthers' new direction.

Peace and Panthers

The Black Panthers were planning a new campaign of their own. On December 12, 1967, Black Panther leader Bobby Seale announced that the Black Panther Party and the Peace and Freedom Party would join forces. The Peace and Freedom Party was a third political party that didn't align with Republicans or Democrats. The party devoted itself entirely to rights movements, most notably women's rights and African American civil rights, and to ending the Vietnam War.

This new alliance marked the Black Panthers' official entry into politics. Before this, the party had focused on community organizing, but now they were ready to change the system from the inside. The Peace and Freedom Party would nominate several Black Panther members for U.S. president in 1968. ∎

Guess Who's Coming to Dinner

Released on December 11, the film *Guess Who's Coming to Dinner*, starring Sidney Poitier, made headlines for its positive depiction of interracial marriage. In the film, an engaged white woman and Black man introduce each other to their families. Their family members disapprove at first, fearing that the couple's children will face discrimination. After seeing how much the two are in love, their families gradually come to accept the marriage. This film reflects the changing attitudes of the time: With *Loving v. Virginia* legalizing interracial marriage across the country just a few months earlier, more Americans were warming to the idea. *Guess Who's Coming to Dinner* won two Academy Awards.

Sidney Poitier and Katharine Houghton starred in *Guess Who's Coming to Dinner*.

Dr. King meets with President Johnson.

The Legacy of 1967 in Civil Rights History

The year 1967 was a year of love, a year of change, and a year of possibility. Americans welcomed many African Americans into government. Walter E. Washington was appointed the first African American mayor of a major American city. Carl Stokes and Richard Hatcher became the first elected mayors of American cities. And Edward W. Brooke took office as the first African American U.S. senator in the 20th century. Thurgood Marshall also took his place as the first African American Supreme Court justice.

Federal law was slowly evolving to embrace civil rights. *Loving v. Virginia* struck down all laws against interracial marriage, meaning that for the first time in American history, people of different races could marry each other without fear of imprisonment.

But as love triumphed at home, America waged a terrible war overseas. The Vietnam War was a costly conflict that unfairly targeted young African

American men and Vietnamese civilians. In the speech "Beyond Vietnam," Dr. King called for the fighting to end. The war cost money, time, and resources that should have been used to help America's poor. President Johnson and the SCLC criticized King for speaking out, but the growing peace movement proved King right.

The anti-war movement, headed by African American civil rights leader James Bevel and the Mobe, grew steadily. San Francisco's Human Be-In kicked off a key strategy of the movement: peaceful demonstrations that involved singing and passing out flowers. This sprouted into the Summer of Love.

Anti-war protesters march to the United Nations headquarters.

King also announced a new campaign: the Poor People's Campaign. He wanted to focus on the economic issues oppressing African Americans, such as housing discrimination and lower wages.

It was these ongoing, systemic economic problems that led to the Long, Hot Summer of '67. While many white activists were enjoying the Summer of Love, Black activists took their protests to the streets in 159 cities. Instead of listening, President Johnson ordered the military to attack U.S. citizens. And when the Kerner Commission found that the American government was to blame for the protests, Johnson wanted to bury the information.

But try as he might, Johnson couldn't stop the nationwide changes that were already in motion. Anti-war protests would continue until every American soldier came home. The Black Panthers began shifting their focus to politics. African Americans were ready to riot in order to enact change. And the Poor People's Campaign was poised to mobilize America's poor across racial and ethnic lines in a way that had never been done before.

No one knew that the next year, 1968, would turn the entire country upside down. Was America ready? ■

Ketanji Brown Jackson

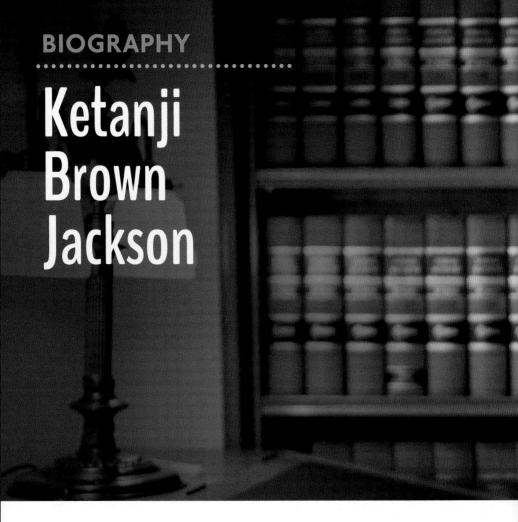

Ketanji Brown Jackson was born in Washington, DC, on September 14, 1970. Her love of law started very young. When she was still a child, her father left his secure job as a history teacher to pursue his dream and enroll in law school.

Jackson remembers her father studying textbooks at the kitchen table. His dedication taught her that no matter what, she should never give up on what she wanted.

Like Thurgood Marshall, the first African American Supreme Court justice, Jackson's parents attended

Ketanji Brown Jackson is the first female African American Supreme Court justice.

historically Black colleges. They raised Ketanji to be proud of her African American **heritage**, and to speak out for what she believed was right.

Inspired by her parents, Jackson became a strong leader. She was class president at Miami Palmetto Senior High School, where she was voted "most likely to succeed" and became a national debate champion.

But when Jackson told her high school counselor that she was going to apply to Harvard University, her counselor advised her to aim lower. Never one to be discouraged, Jackson applied anyway—and got in. As an

In 1988, Jackson, a high school senior, poses for the yearbook.

undergraduate at Harvard, she led protests, studied government, and graduated with highest honors. After working for *Time* magazine, she attended Harvard Law School.

In 2009, President Barack Obama appointed her to the United States Sentencing Commission, an important judicial body that decides how long to sentence people for federal crimes. This commission is crucial, because African Americans often receive longer sentences for committing

"Our children are telling me that they see now, more than ever, that, here in America, anything is possible."

—KENTANJI BROWN JACKSON

President Joe Biden nominated Jackson to the Supreme Court.

Jackson is sworn in as a U.S. District Court judge in 2013.

the same crimes as white Americans. During her time on the commission, Jackson successfully helped get reduced sentences for those who committed nonviolent crimes.

Although she worked for short periods for private law firms, Jackson dedicated the majority of her career to public service. She worked tirelessly, like Thurgood Marshall, to defend the rights of minorities and of other people who suffered discrimination.

On March 26, 2013, she became a judge on the United States District Court for the District of Columbia. During her time on the bench, she handed down many decisions that bravely opposed the racist and discriminatory policies of the Trump administration. She defended the rights of federal employees to collectively bargain for better pay. She also worked to keep the Department of Homeland Security from deporting noncitizens.

On June 14, 2021, Jackson was confirmed as a circuit judge for the U.S. Court of Appeals for the DC Circuit. This is the second-most influential U.S. court, after the Supreme Court. A year later, on June 30, 2022, she was sworn in as a Supreme Court justice. ■

TIMELINE

The Year in Civil Rights

1967

MARCH 6

Legendary boxer Muhammad Ali learns that he will have to serve in the Vietnam War.

JANUARY 10

Edward W. Brooke takes his seat as the first African American in the U.S. Senate from Massachusetts.

FEBRUARY 28

The U.S. government finds seven of the 18 men indicted for the murder of three young activists in Mississippi guilty of civil rights violations.

APRIL 4

Dr. Martin Luther King, Jr., delivers his iconic anti-war speech, "Beyond Vietnam."

MAY 2

The Black Panthers protest the Mulford Act in the California State Capitol, carrying guns.

JUNE 12

The Supreme Court rules in the *Loving v. Virginia* case that interracial marriage is legal.

JULY 23

The Detroit Rebellion, or the Detroit Uprising, the bloodiest protest of the summer, begins.

AUGUST 30

Thurgood Marshall is officially confirmed as the first African American Supreme Court justice in American history.

SEPTEMBER 6

Walter E. Washington is appointed mayor of Washington, DC, becoming the first African American mayor of any major American city.

OCTOBER 21

One of the most significant demonstrations against the Vietnam War takes place in Washington, DC.

NOVEMBER 27

Dr. King meets with the SCLC to discuss the Poor People's Campaign.

DECEMBER 11

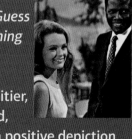

The film *Guess Who's Coming to Dinner*, starring Sidney Poitier, is released, showing a positive depiction of interracial marriage.

GLOSSARY

abolish (uh-BAH-lish) to put an end to something officially

activist (AK-tuh-vist) a person who works to bring about political or social change

affirmative action (uh-FUR-muh-tiv AK-shuhn) the use of policies, legislation, programs, and procedures to improve the educational or employment opportunities of certain groups to remedy the effects of long-standing discrimination against these groups

amendment (uh-MEND-muhnt) a change that is made to a law or a legal document

appeal (uh-PEEL) an application to a higher court for a change in a legal decision

attorney general (uh-TUR-nee JEN-ur-uhl) the chief law officer of a nation or state who represents the government in court and serves as its principal legal adviser

boycott (BOI-kaht) a refusal to buy something or do business with someone as a protest

cease-fire (SEES-fire) a temporary pause during a war, usually to allow peace talks to take place

civil rights (SIV-uhl rites) the individual rights that all members of a democratic society have to freedom and equal treatment under the law

civilian (suh-VIL-yuhn) a person who is not a member of the military or police or firefighting force

Communist (KAHM-yuh-nist) an advocate of communism, which is a system in which goods are owned in common and are available to all as needed

covenant (KUHV-uh-nuhnt) a formal and often legal agreement to do or avoid a certain thing

discrimination (dis-krim-uh-NAY-shuhn) prejudiced or unfair behavior toward others based on differences in such things as race, gender, or age

draft a system in which young people are required to join the armed forces of a country for a period of service

economic (ek-uh-NAH-mik) of or having to do with the way money, resources, and services are used in a society

federal (FED-ur-uhl) having to do with the national government, as opposed to state or local government

felony (FEL-uh-nee) a serious crime, such as murder

heritage (HER-i-tij) traditions and beliefs that a country or society considers an important part of its history

hippie (HIP-ee) a person, especially one in the 1960s, who rejects traditional values and opposes violence and war

indict (in-DITE) to officially charge someone with a crime

integrate (IN-ti-grate) to make facilities or an organization open to people of all races and ethnic groups

Jim Crow (jim kro) the former practice of segregating Black people in the United States

Ku Klux Klan (KOO kluks KLAN) a secret organization in the United States that uses threats and violence to achieve its goal of white supremacy; also called the Klan or the KKK

legislation (lej-is-LAY-shuhn) a law or set of laws that have been proposed or made

lynching (LIN-ching) a sometimes public murder by a group of people, often involving hanging

Nation of Islam (NAY-shuhn uhv IZ-lahm) an African American movement and organization that combines the religion of Islam with Black Nationalist ideas

prestigious (pres-TIJ-uhs) commanding great respect and status by being successful, powerful, rich, or famous

psychedelic (sye-kuh-DE-lik) of, relating to, characteristic of, or being the period of the mid to late 1960s that is associated with the drug culture at that time

racism (RAY-si-zuhm) thinking that a particular race is better than others or treating people unfairly or cruelly because of their race

segregation (seg-ruh-GAY-shuhn) the act or practice of keeping people or groups apart

sit-in (SIT-in) a form of protest in which demonstrators occupy a place, refusing to leave until their demands are met

stereotype (STER-ee-oh-tipe) a widely held but overly simplistic idea, opinion, or image of a person, group, or thing

systemic (si-STE-mik) fundamental to a predominant social, economic, or political practice

unconstitutional (uhn-kahn-sti-TOO-shuh-nuhl) not in keeping with the basic principles or laws set forth in the U.S. Constitution

BIBLIOGRAPHY

DeSilver, Drew. "Who's Poor in America? 50 Years into the 'War on Poverty,' a Data Portrait." *Pew Research Center*, Pew Research Center, 13 Jan. 2014, www.pewresearch.org/fact-tank/2014/01/13/whos-poor-in-america-50-years-into-the-war-on-poverty-a-data-portrait/.

Gillon, Steven M. "Why a 1967 Federal Report on Urban Riots Suppressed Its Own Expert Findings." *HISTORY*, 31 Jan. 2019, www.history.com/news/race-riots-kerner-commission-findings-suppressed-lbj.

"National Mobilization Committee to End the War in Vietnam Records (DG 075), Swarthmore College Peace Collection." *Swarthmore.edu*, 2009, www.swarthmore.edu/library/peace/DG051-099/dg075nmc.htm.

"Spring Mobilization to End the War in 1967 – World Peace through Technology." *Peace Tour*, 15 Apr. 2017, peacetour.org/spring-mobilization-1967/.

"Vietnam War | the Martin Luther King, Jr., Research and Education Institute." *Stanford.edu*, 2006, kinginstitute.stanford.edu/encyclopedia/vietnam-war.

Peaceful protestors call for an end to the Vietnam War.

INDEX

About the Author

Jay Leslie is a writer who cares about revolution. Her other books include *Who Did It First? 50 Politicians, Activists and Entrepreneurs Who Revolutionized the World* and *Game, Set, Sisters! The Story of Venus and Serena Williams*. Connect with Jay at www.Jay-Leslie.com.

PHOTO CREDITS